Daily writing projects come as no surprise, and seldom offer any. The products of self-imposed and regulated poetic labor often read like not much more than that: output. *Diurne*, which presents itself as the record of one poet's ritual writing practice ("a line each hour of waking / a poem each day of making"), is among the great exceptions. Whip-smart, allusive, aphoristic, cheekily instructive, shot with lyricism, endlessly playful, intimate, anxious, and often laugh-out-loud funny, *Diurne* achieves with great grace and relative efficiency what the best examples of its subgenre have to offer: it limns a sense of consciousness through whatever is at hand as it places the noteworthy on equal footing with the banal. But what truly distinguishes *Diurne* is the affective force with which it undertakes its given task: "This is a poem written under duress," the text professes, and there is never any doubt of it. Rooted in confusions of desire and of the work of being one among many; in questions of subjectivity, economy, and ecology, *Diurne* drags the reader through its divagations in such a fever that it should probably go home, relax, take the rest of the day off…**From where I'm standing, it's pretty much a masterpiece**.

*—from the Sunken Garden Poetry Prize citation*
*by award judge Timothy Donnelly*

T0083511

## SUNKEN GARDEN POETRY AT HILL-STEAD MUSEUM

Sunken Garden Poetry began in 1992 in Farmington, Connecticut, with a single poetry reading in the magical setting of Hill-Stead Museum's Sunken Garden, drawing huge crowds even that first year. Since then the annual series has become one of the premiere and best-loved venues for poetry in the country, featuring the top tier of American poets as well as emerging and student writers from the region. From its inception more than twenty-five years ago, this poetry festival has given equal weight to the quality of text and the poet's ability to deliver an engaging, powerful, and entertaining experience in the unique theater of the Sunken Garden.

Out of the festival have grown competitions, year-round workshops and events, and an educational outreach to Hartford high schools. And while centered at Hill-Stead—with its beautiful views, Colonial Revival house, and priceless collection of Impressionist paintings—Sunken Garden Poetry now engages an ever-wider audience through a growing online presence; an online poetry journal, *Theodate* (now found at hillstead.org); public radio broadcasts; and an annual chapbook prize, co-published by Tupelo Press.

### Sunken Garden Chapbook Poetry Prize

2019
*Diurne* by Kristin George Bagdanov
Selected by Timothy Donnelly

2018
*Flight* by Chaun Ballard
Selected by Major Jackson

2017
*Ordinary Misfortunes* by Emily Jungmin Yoon
Selected by Maggie Smith

2016
*Feed* by Suzanne Parker
Selected by Jeffrey Levine and Cassandra Cleghorn

2015
*Fountain and Furnace* by Hadara Bar-Nadav
Selected by Peter Stitt

2014
*We Practice For It* by Ted Lardner
Selected by Mark Doty

# diurne

Kristin George Bagdanov

TUPELO PRESS
North Adams, Massachusetts

Library of Congress Catalog-in-Publication data available upon request.
ISBN paperback: ISBN-13: 978-1-946482-28-0

Cover and text designed by Howard Klein.

Cover art: Pecos Pryor, "2 Years: Sifted Pencil Shavings." Copyright 2018 Pecos Pryor (pecospryor.com). Used with permission.

First edition: September 2019

Tupelo Press
P.O. Box 1767
North Adams, Massachusetts 01247
Telephone: 413-664-9611 / Fax: 413-664-9711
editor@tupelopress.org / www.tupelopress.org

Tupelo Press is an award-winning independent literary press that publishes fine fiction, nonfiction, and poetry in books that are a joy to hold as well as read. Tupelo Press is a registered 501(c)(3) nonprofit organization, and we rely on public support to carry out our mission of publishing extraordinary work that may be outside the realm of large commercial publishers. Financial donations are welcome and are tax deductible.

*For all the creatures I've met in the meantime*

ACKNOWLEDGEMENTS

This book would not exist without the Vermont Studio Center. In July 2017, with support from the Henry David Thoreau fellowship, I set out to write *Diurne*. The project unfolded at a rate of one line per waking hour, a durational writing practice that would not have been possible were it not for the time and space provided by VSC. I also want to thank the writers and artists I met there, whose conversations, poems, paintings, and gestures shaped this project and, in some cases, appear within it. My gratitude especially for the talented poets Liz Johnson, Kate Gibbel, Casey Patrick, Kelin Loe, Franny Choi, and Ilya Kaminsky as well as the many incredible visual artists at VSC, particularly the BABS set. Thank you to Pecos Pryor, whose art graces the cover of this book. The image, "Two Years: Sifted Pencil Shavings," was produced through a method of accumulation, duration, and ritual and is the perfect complement for *Diurne*. My gratitude to Timothy Donnelly and Tupelo Press for their work in selecting, editing, and producing this project. And finally, thank you, Levi, for building a life with me, line by line, hour by hour.

A LINE EACH HOUR OF WAKING / A POEM EACH DAY OF MAKING

1

In the unlit lampshade, a stillness

I satisfy my need by defining my need. My desire is everyone else telling me what to want to be.

The heart beats by seeing its EKG saying so. Cardiac event recorder in which the horizon is always rupture without revelation.

Undertow pulls the legs which way the arms this way. Image of contra without diction.

If social being is consciousness, then these rocks I cut my feet against, my blood in the water, makes this, too

Two waves break against each other, neither the aggressor. Both make a mouthful of salt.

I have gone into a wave laughing. I have seen how calm the explanation.

This is not an attempt at immediacy. This is a poem written under duress. I'm not authentic but an aura lingers at my lips.

This mouth imbibes microplastics and runoff. I swallow with and without knowledge. This is not a treatise or confession. Both have their states and I am neither one of them.

Mineral made bone made knowledge. Open your hand. Find it a shovel; give it a gun. Callus the space between.

I am told the mess of the subject is what makes a poem interesting

Cf. the grasp of hoof vs. hand

To that end, I am structuring my feeling. At this end, I make space for each hour to speak.

I wrote that earlier but out of order. I hadn't considered how it wanted to be beheld.

My desire is everyone else

2

Every poem satisfies its need by producing another. *Want*, a definition that ends with *see also:*

We are tired of defining ourselves. By *ourselves* I mean all the bodies that have been classified as life/living by a system that prizes *bio* over *geo*. How to become unliving without death as demarcation?

Emergence of form in fern: spore structure not underhanded but unhandled

I am told details make a poem *relatable*. Condensation of mind into image that is not so much *mine* as *ours*.

Subjects of history said *yes fractal, no still life*. Montage more real than portrait. Why plunge into wanting when it already scums the surface?

I want the pretense of presence. As in: can you hear the river at my feet can you feel the tick in my thigh? *Prove it on the pulse,* said someone.

The residue of my moment: all pith. Nectar a method of making sweet from sweat.

I am told no one wants to read a poem that keeps reminding them it is a poem. You should take a nap instead.

When I say *immediate* I mean the substance at hand: sky, river, human, car, finch. *See also:* DDT, Solo cup, exhaust.

When I am unmade: teeth radiating their signature after history. Postpartum of the world finally giving up its human.

I am afraid there is not enough personal information in this poem. My credit card # is 4060-5678-6500-8040 EXP: 06/22 CCV: 866. I get points for every $.

Possible futures:

One in which dogs are drinking beer on the lawn of a small town

One that defines the human by sealing it shut: flesh into stone, which we say we are least like

One that turns earth outside-in, burial of shit that drifts on the surface

Method: I pulse the structure that subsumes me

TO BECOME WHOLE WITHOUT FIRST BECOMING *WHO*

3

Species barrier also a binding. Small deaths daily keep us close.

Method: I divide my desire by the background extinction rate

Antarctic ice shelf Larsen C calved an iceberg the size of Delaware today. This is the first time I have really thought about Delaware.

I'm not a good runner but I do it almost daily. Sometimes I walk if no one is looking. I hate the sound of unmediated breath.

Also today, humans formed a human chain off the coast of FL to save someone from a rip current. The man who started it said he got the idea from watching ants. Surplus populations are often compared to insects. As in, "They were crawling all over the city." In this case, that was not the case.

This is where I tell you nothing is unmediated

I am tired of language-as-messenger getting shot for not being the thing itself

Humans are also building a clock to measure 10,000 years: The Long Now. 10,000 is a biblical number. It means "too much." It means "line between human and god." Not enough for Frost, who wanted ten thousand *thousand* apples.

Extinction is the death of populations. No intimacy of that last guttural breath. No mass last rites.

Pre-petrified bodies a half-billion years ago. Hot perspiring heaps used skin as binding agent, zone of inclusion.

The zone of exclusion around Fukushima Daiichi is 20km wide

Soft parts go first. Flesh peats into coal into engine into smoke. The center burns red.

Everyone is waiting for this poem to align

Roof shingles and a broken window. Moss and rust. These are images you might find on iStock when you search for "barn" or "countryside."

We produce each other constantly. A sentence is a method of growing toward.

If you get caught in a rip current, you should swim parallel to the shore. That is what ants would do.

A fragment is not as radical as people think. It is nostalgic for its whole, always longing to return.

4

Make space for chokecherry, which prefers to stretch out and root deep. This may sound trite under current conditions.

The Paleolithic handprints in Pech Merle cave were measured and determined to be women's. I was told, "The first artists were women" as an encouragement. All I see is evidence of pressure. The fingers spread wide to grasp their own mark.

Suction of wet shirt on skin

You are not overhearing me

Do all the poets who write about sex no longer have mothers?

He became a gesture that moved me

*Certain stones which have the figures of animals inside and outside,* said someone

Civilization as achievement: non-barbaric

This poem is civilized. It is following the rules I have established.

The rule now would be to break it. Everyone is waiting for this poem to turn.

Surplus populations are often referred to as strays. Cleaning a city makes it attractive to foreign capital. Ownership being next to godliness.

A city is built upon many deaths. A population, once extinct, validates the civilizing mechanism.

Make live / let die / kill / erase

Sever part from whole to find what haunts. Fragment, a shape of ruin. Edge that erases the memory of center.

I thought he was a theory that proved me

*Identity is a wound*, said someone

In the interim, the poem makes its own method

5

I woke up into it. I woke up and it was already burning.

Once I saw the clouds outside, I changed my mind

Writing is not therapy so why do I keep bringing up my mother? I am writing to not-her.

*The soul is the form of a natural body which potentially has life,* said someone

Are you buying this?

If this was a job, every segment would equal an hour. The minimum wage in CA is $10/hr. A living wage is $13.21/hr.

Hourly made: a wage poem

The performance review of this poem would say: Not very efficient but very dependable. Could be a better team player. Manages expectations.

Catered lunches humanize the workplace. Free childcare and showers. You never have to leave.

Red slug on the sidewalk / Will I step around?

People want to care about a poem. They need a reason to do so. Please rate your satisfaction with this poem from 1-5: _____.

Taylor (of the –ism) wanted to be a choreographer. He loved the ballet. The synchronous pulsing of slender pink legs.

Please text your comments and complaints to: (949) 246-5417. SMS charges will apply according to who carries you.

In return I will labor more affectively

I am overhearing a red-winged black bird. A trill that sounds like it's already underwater.

This would make $160 dollars. If I was living, $211.36.

I HAVEN'T BEEN WRITING ON MY LUNCH BREAK
BECAUSE I DON'T HAVE A JOB

6

My condition is walking through the street with some people yelling.
Waiting in a back room with no one crying.

Where do stones come from? Aristotle's theory of elemental
transmutation: the power of the heavens as efficient cause.

Method: outrun mosquitos

Golden snail on the trail / Will I step around?

*What happens to water and earth also happens to animals and plants, since by a
hidden power of material, the time, or the place, they are completely disintegrated
or converted into stone,* said someone.

I manage my carbon footprint by holding my breath

Mosquitos are a surplus population expressed via disease vectors which
have direction and magnitude. Not too long ago They used organic
phosphates such as Malathion to eliminate them for not too long. There
were many unintended casualties, such as the Mediterranean fruit fly. An
enzyme in mammalian livers renders the chemical impotent. However,
this is not always the case, especially in cases where there are already
other phosphates at work. In those cases, they get off on each other and
potently fuck your mammalian liver.

If you would like to get in on the ground floor of this poem, please
email your ceiling to kgeorgebagdanov@gmail.com

"They" means mgmt.

After I graduated from college in 2009, I took two part-time internships with non-profit organizations. At one, I entered data for 6 weeks for a $600 stipend. I had to slow down to earn it. At the other, I worked for 8 weeks for $2,000 and my boss asked me to take the company Blackberry home "just in case" he needed me when I wasn't there. There were 144 hrs/wk when I wasn't there, 16 of which I was entering data.

This is not a self-regulating poem. It cannot dissolve its oppositions.

*A self-organizing system feeds upon noise,* said someone

I was hungry and ate a donut, which is something I normally don't let myself do

In any case, I said I didn't feel comfortable taking such a fancy phone home to the house I shared with seven people. I started losing my keys and spilling my coffee to demonstrate my incompetence.

Who gets to live a livable life?

Measurements make the undead into deities and dead into numbers

Ghosts do not waste their time

7

As if my brain were styrofoam: a hangover

I put a dollar in the machine and receive four quarters in return. A decent exchange rate.

Often, the most pressing question an adult will have for a child is, "How old are you?"

Apologies in advance for not shaving, is something I often say. It implies the situation is irregular.

Ticks corral humans, spreading fear through word-of-mouth.

As a child, I did not enjoy talking to adults, who were always bending over with bad breath

This poem is a study in time mgmt. "99% of life is just showing up" say a lot of people. Corporations call this "presentism," in which the laborer's body is at a desk but they're flarfing or facebooking or meditating instead of making memos.

The Big One is Lyme. Also Rocky Mtn. Spotted Fever, Tulaquemia, Ehrlichiosis, Babesiosis.

*Parasite*: In ancient Greece, a person who ate at the table of the wealthy and repaid them in flattery, not coin

Two intersecting spheres are never on equal terms. One limns the other's edge before subsuming it.

Country songs often use "checking for ticks" as a means of instigating intercourse. The erotics of inspection.

The "reality principle" is when you give up bad sex today for great sex tomorrow. In other words, self-denial makes us real.

Sweating as an index of effort

In the 70s, some people thought machines would allow humans to work less. The main problem being how to find hobbies for all that free time.

Method: slow data

I am looking for the aurora borealis

Moon rim with heat stitch // cloud in my lungs / cloud on my tongue

8

How to live inside the waking thought without question

I'm not trying to express myself. I'm just trying to mark the time.

This poem is 99% humidity

Does sitting under a canopy of trees and watching the rain make me
a caricature?

How to register the recording of the sensation of the event: the new
new new realism made old again. Photos of other people photographing
*Mona Lisa.*

Certified Forest Therapists can instruct you on "forest bathing," which
is a metaphor for immersing oneself in one's natural environment. The
Association of Nature and Forest Therapy (ANFT) hopes to certify and
train 250 new guides next year. The average forest bather sees a reduction
of blood pressure by 7 mmHg / 4 hours. The average forest sees an
increase in human pressure of 2,000lbs / 4 hours.

Mediation as middle mgmt.

This poem is task-oriented

I just spent 15 minutes trying to take a selfie of myself working on
this poem. I did not end up posting the photo due to concerns re:
narcissism. You can follow me on Instagram at @KristinGeorgeB.

Looking as if you aren't looking is the original lyric pose: the
self(ie) overheard

Method: impersonal intimacy

The problem isn't not being able to live with yourself. It's being able to.

Each task is an aspect of certain relations and cannot be rendered through a prefab structure of meaning

Meaning, I'm waiting for this poem to mirror me. The illusion of unity in the subject is what makes a poem pleasurable.

When tasked with the choice, I found it wasn't one

9

Gravel on my tongue / consequence of wanting / the thing / that turns
me / to stone

I'm back on my regularly programmed schedule today

Medusa, whose beauty was petrifying, turned subjects into objects that
also could not shield themselves from eternity's gaze

Shirts that say "I went to Vermont and all I got was this lousy shirt" make
great pre-recorded jokes for casual Fridays. *Lousy*, as in: infested with lice,
also called the parasite of the poor.

If you would like to purchase this poem, please Venmo its value to
@KristinGeorgeB

The liberation of not making a living. Of living a making.

Ideal schedule: Wake between 7-8am, go to sleep between 10-11pm.
This ensures 8 hours of rest and 16 hours of productive making, or, two
workdays in one.

As children, my sisters and I shampooed each other's hair in the bathtub.
My mother used a fine metal comb that made my scalp ache. The lice
she found she did not eat, which distinguishes humans from our primate
cousins. The eros of inspection.

His mind pressing against mine

Lyric as personal branding

The basilisk features prominently in bestiaries but is excluded from lapidaries, even though it might answer the nagging question of "Where do stones come from?"

Lousy flea-rat-boat assemblages suppressed populations and redistributed land. All the dead who couldn't manage their property.

The crustacean with its one heavy claw—remnant of world unplagued by symmetry

I was asked how long I spend composing each segment / wage / task. I said it is difficult to assess, as the indirect labor must be compounded annually at a rate of 4%, while the affective labor varies with the moon cycle.

Wife of Lot made mineral from her gaze. Worth more in salt than flesh.

Whether one element can be transmuted into another is basic alchemy

The person writing this poem is more put together than I am

POEM A WOOL / THAT PULLS / WATER FROM AIR / YOU THOUGHT
WAS DRY

10

I see the signs / of age encroach // little roach on my hand / fat moth beneath my chin

Each poetry book contest costs approx. $30. That's three wage-segments' worth. 300-1,500 people enter each contest, depending on the reputation and marketing skills of the press. Also, the judge. So, your statistical chance of winning is 0.3% – 0.06%.

In the interim, I mostly walked, which was not an efficient use of time. It was for the mosquitos, however.

There are no great poets without great critics

Notions of totality are upsetting for many

If you have trouble filling your time, interest curation services are available to assist

Still better odds than the Mega Millions Lottery, which are 1 in 258.9 million. However, in one case you end up with mega millions, and the other, a book of poetry.

This poem does not represent the significance of existence

I'm told that admitting your failures does not lead to success. No one wants the thing that no one else wants because desire is socially constructed through erotic economics.

[Insert what Latour says about totalities leading to totalitarianism]

Make an effigy of your mind / and find how hands / work under pressure / how the match breaks and breaks

What imagination desires into fact. What it rewrites in secret.

Once you're an established poet, it's best to produce a book every 2-3 years. This timeline accommodates tenure clocks and helps ensure you won't become an erasure.

This poem is not trying to describe what is or what will be

Men who still like Kant

"A high number of quality submissions" and an invitation to try again next year.

11

Now I only think of you when I realize I haven't

It is not so much the object of pleasure as the aura it produces

Hours when clouds are omens vs. shade

We read our future through animal bodies

As a child I helped my mother build trick boxes for a magician who signed her checks in disappearing ink

"The nymph must lose her female friend / if more admired than she"— Cowper explains why yr posse shld b less attractive than u

Birds bathing in dirt or growing from it. The magic of spontaneous generation.

I tweeted that Cowper bit earlier and wrote it down here b/c I think it's my funniest tweet

The correlation between academics and people who like magic

*A mutation occurs when the ionization of an atom changes the genetic coding of a cell, producing a new reproductive outcome,* said someone.

Mutants are often cast as villains. Except when they're heroes.

The standard background radiation rate is approx. 360 millirems / yr

By splitting a fish in half and placing it on a photographic plate, u can read how fucked u r in millirems: a radio-autograph.

My ears are still ringing with it

A bull was found grazing in the exclusion zone around Chernobyl which made people hopeful so they captured and bred and tested it

I always found the trick more magical once I knew its mechanism

Please tweet these lines and follow me @KristinGeorgeB. All opinions are not my own.

IN CASE OF EMERGENCY, THIS POEM CAN SHIELD YOU
FROM APPROX. .00001 MILLIREMS

12

Hand that holds its own / a sketch of loss in charcoal

Even a gesture leaves its mark. My hands still heavy with his.

River that smells of the sea toward which it's flowing

I just showered with a moth and the feeling was mutual

For example, while sitting contemplatively by the river, an oldish man
and his dog started talking to me. The dog did not say much. I did not
want to talk to this strange man upon a slick rock beside the white river,
so I folded my arms across my chest as indication. By the time I sidled
and skittled around him, I had learned more of him than you have of me:
how many fish he had caught and when (with pics), how he helped his
friend get off drugs, when he injured his back (September 5, 2001) and
how many surgeries and how he wanted to work but couldn't and how
many vehicles he had and how old his dog was (9 but people think he's a
puppy).

Before Pasteur ruined spontaneous generation with biogenesis, maggots
grew from flesh, lice from fur, poems from spirits, life from death

You could say I'm a "spiritual" person

*Omne vivum ex vivo,* he said

Half-hoping someone will see me being thoughtful

You could "say" I'm not "in it" for the "money"

I try not to generalize my private anxieties

"I" in the past tense

Everyone seems proud of someone for something on Facebook

I am trying to stay solvent. Solve the mess of myself before ruining
anyone else.

"I" in the conditional

This poem is desperate for an alibi

I take the world inside me / I take the world inside me & make nothing
// of it. No miracle / of transformation / matter made matter stays
matter stays / me

Eventually we put our hands up. Eventually we take the moon in our
mouths and say nothing.

13

I want to take a day off but I won't start accruing vacation until I've been here for three months

My body refuses to learn its edges

I am not the first person you would notice in a crowd

I haven't written about my mother for a while. Maybe I solved it. Maybe this poem is my mother.

If I had an avg. office job, 40hrs/wk w/ 2wks PTO, I would accrue .038hrs of PTO/hr. For example, so far today I would have earned 0.19hrs or 11.5 min. of PTO.

I'm not sure which crisis this poem is responding to

Men in my MFA program who said every poem was about being a poem

Not everyone will use the OED to read your poem

We've all written a poem about murmuration

I'm floating in the river but can't stop thinking about my thighs rubbing together

I'm not making anything new here

After I pull the grass from my hair / After I make my hands a garden / After I watch it disappear /

I'm not completing any more tasks until I start earning some damn vacation time

An accrual poem

In 2015, 55% of Americans who accrued vacation didn't use all of it. A lot of people like to hoard their vacation days so that when they leave their job they can "cash out" and give themselves a little bonus for never missing work. Corporations prefer to call vacation days "Paid Time Off" so that you forget that vacation is the opposite of working. Vacation, as in, vacate: to be empty, free, etc.

*My mother is a fish*, said someone

I have earned a 38 min. nap

14

It's Sunday so this poem will have an agenda

I'm going to tell you about nuclear waste

Hanford, WA: Home of the Trinity "test" bomb and the Nagasaki bomb. After the Cold War ended there remained 53 million gallons of high-level waste (HLW) to deal with. That's enough waste to fill over 1 million bathtubs, which it probably has. Most is stored underground in containers that occasionally leak into the soil and water supply. *Matter without place,* said someone.

On my birthday this year, a tunnel in Hanford collapsed. They fixed it by filling the hole with 550 cubic yards of soil (about 183 large dumpsters).

Cow stench in my lungs / hooftench on my tongue

In its hay day, Hanford routinely released radionuclides into the air, which leached into the grass into the cows into the milk into the people into the streams into the fish into the people

Here is a sampling of the radionuclides released into the air around Hanford from 1944-1972:^

| radionuclides | amount released (curies) | half-life | known effects on humans |
|---|---|---|---|
| Iodine-131* | 740,000 | 8 days | Thyroid cancer, esp. in children |
| Tritium (H-3)** | 200,000 | 12 years | Cancer, mutations, especially in developing fetuses, as Tritium behaves like water |

| | | | |
|---|---|---|---|
| Strontium-90★★★ | 64 | 29 years | Bone cancer, leukemia, lung cancer; behaves like calcium and attaches easily to bone |
| Cesium-137★★★★ | 42 | 30 years | Cancer, especially in soft tissue and muscle |
| Plutonium -239★★★★★ | 1.8 | 24,000 years | Moves into bones, liver, and other organs, where it emits alpha radiation for decades. Common cancers incl: lung, liver, and bone sarcoma |

^ *While smaller releases have continued since 1972, the Congressional mandate for the Hanford Health Information Network (HHIN) limits the Network to providing information about the releases of radioactive materials from 1944 to 1972,* said someone.

★ In 1949, a secret U.S. Air Force experiment at Hanford released between 7,000 and 12,000 curies of iodine-131. This was called the "Green Run" because it involved a processing "run" of uranium fuel that had only been cooled for 16 days and was therefore "green," which is to say, "new" or "inexperienced." At Three-Mile Island, only 17 curies of Iodine-131 were released from the core. We call this progress.

★★Commonly found in drinking water

★★★Between 1949 to 1956 the Mayak nuclear production site in the former Soviet Union dumped approx. 76 million cubic meters of radioactive waste into the Techa River (enough to fill more than 30,000 Olympic-sized swimming pools), a large portion of which was Strontium-90. The plant continued to dump at least 30 million cubic meters of untreated nuclear waste into the river from 2001 to 2004. It is still in operation.

****The "fingerprint" of the recent Fukushima Daiichi disaster, which has been reported by citizen scientists to be present in fish on the Oregon coast. Official government sources have neither confirmed nor denied these findings.

*****See Ginsberg's "Plutonian Ode"

*To date, there has been no practical need for a final HLW repository*, said someone

Return of the repressed

In CA, there are 3,390 metric tons of used nuclear fuel being stored here and there

Cocooning is when reactors are demolished and buried. Only when they are safe to handle will they emerge from the chrysalis.

Caterpillars spend anywhere from 7 days to over a year in their cocoons

Every thing is some thing's cocoon

While inside the chrysalis the caterpillar dissolves into a puddle of goo. Tests show that the post-goo butterfly remembers things from its pre-goo life, giving us an idea about how memory and form and matter work.

We spend our whole lives trying to reform the past

LIKE YOU, I SEE A HOLE AND WANT TO FILL IT / LIKE ME, YOU SEE
A BODY AND WANT TO BURY IT

15

I am on the verge of waking. I find an edge inside myself and push.

I hold my ache underwater / It stops twitching

Rain relocates the shit at my feet to someone else's street. For instance, runoff, chockfull of pesticides, flows into the ocean and begins a process call *eutrophication* ("well nourished"). Algae get fat off phosphates then die. Bacteria eat their corpses and use up all the oxygen. From above, dead zones look like oases in an expanse of uninhabitable blue. Everything in the ocean is looking up from below.

My mother just texted to see if I could talk but I said I was in the middle of something, which I am

Remediation is a process by which exposure to radiation is reduced through the treatment of contaminated soil, groundwater, and surface water. The goal is to return the site to its original state. Edenic aspirations.

Each remediation produces more materials that require remediation

"zero waste"

The terms "cleanup," "rehabilitation," and "restoration" are often used in public discussions of remediation.

Every good poet needs a pen pal. Please write to me at 1514 F St. Apt. #3 Sacramento, CA 95814.

After Fukushima: *We want to return it to a safe state...We promised the local people that we would recover the site and make it a safe ground again,* said someone

A common question is: "How clean is clean?"

There are no subtleties and niceties waiting for excavation here

Certain government bodies decide what the acceptable levels of toxicity are for its citizenry. In other words, they establish *a permanent ration of collective standardized poisoning,* said someone.

Desserts named after disasters: 1. Mudslide Pie 2. Ice Cream Blizzard 3. Molten Lava Cake 4._____

This poem is a physical relation between physical things. Fugitive form in a world of hostile data.

Who will remediate the meteors?

16

I woke up laughing

A good one-liner is hard to find

Bill Gates walks into a bar and the average income rises from $50k
to $5bill

A lesson on averages vs. distribution

In the U.S., 2,334 people make an avg. of $88.7 mil./yr.

When I die I'm not sure I want to be liquefied, even though it is
eco-friendly

Wet slug on the path / maybe it's taking a bath

Even distribution in a world of uneven development

I should have written a manifesto instead

Repeal & Replace = Cease & Seize

Often I write between the hours. I will make an appendix of middle
time & surplus lines.

A WI company offers employees an implant so they can make copies and
buy snacks

Men who neg women by forgetting their names

I need to establish a better epistolary record

The company says employees are "lining up" for the technology

Make me a chip that can get me out of this line, I say

Quiescent fields menace production. Give the fold its due. Break the
   plow if you have to.

Smoke hissing off a log still wet with yesterday

17

I wake to a mouth wanting me

Who sang the sorrows of whose changing face

This poem is wasteful. I should start recycling.

You can watch silent videos of atomic bombs exploding on various deserts and atolls on Youtube. Researchers at Lawrence Livermore National Laboratory are digitizing our nuclear unconscious.

My jaw aches with rain. I conjure you coming close, my chin an apple in your palm.

In 1963, They agreed to a "partial" test ban which can be summarized as "out of sight out of mind." An article ends: "If we're not careful, the more powerful nuclear weapons of today could cut short our reign as the dominant species on earth."

Decomposed line: attempoem unduress

A man in a small-town coffee shop who is the age of the U.S. president says: "The hunkiest, muscliest, hot male porn star wrestler who didn't start out as a male...it's more fluid. Have you seen *Transparent*? It's so weird how we divide ourselves."

A new red spot on my softening gut

Come, let us make each other strange again

Cobras coiled in chip cans. Soft-shelled turtles stuffed in styrofoam. Exotic international exchange.

As a citizen, she is a commodity of that world

This is my first rodeo

This is my animal longing. Rough snout, root deep.

Here is a small thing / that measures no / thing

WHO ARE YOUR COMPANION SPECIES?

18

I wake without hunger. I wake knowing it will come.

The scent of shit disguised by pine

Many have already experienced the apocalypse. They live in the after
while others build their houses on the beach.

Once or twice in her life / a woman is gutted / like a fish

Please do not read between the lines

My heart a cloister the rain cannot reach

*Hell no, we won't glow*, they said

At a time like this it is hard to even pleasure oneself

The world, it seems, cannot be said

After we destroyed Hiroshima, the first forms of life to emerge
were mushrooms. They feasted on Iodine-131, Stontium-90, and
Plutonium-239. This phenomenon can be classed under radioecology.
No rainbow in the sky, the glow of the heavens brought low.

This poem is tactical

Each encounter a contamination, which is to say, skin was made
impervious by men and modernity. We need help to survive.

All the things that cannot live without first being burned to the ground

Scale as symptom of capitalism. Porta-poem.

This poem might be salvageable. I take what I can and I leave what might give me tetanus. Pick clean the teeth and the hips, pull out the DNA & IUD. Shape them into something new.

I pull an equation from the air

I write what I do not know

19

I need help

subject verb object

how about this?

don't touch me

buy my time

are babies memes?

die, urn, die

end hedgehog hegemony

capitalism isn't casual

garbage of pigeons

kettle of vultures

storage device full

the gag economy

owned & operated

speaks, is spoken

sorry about this

I feel better (thanks)

COME, WRECK ME

20

The architecture of your hands makes me firm again / builds me up
from the heap I've been

I monitor my mistakes, measure them by the pound. I mold them whole
before me and forget who is the monstrous one.

No origin or end. Just the middle ever expanding, the dénouement
always one car chase away.

Clicking in a bush which could be insect or machine or human

How many miles = happiness? 65 so far this month which is not enough

If I'm candid about my mental health will I sell more books? i.e. the
hundreds of times I've ███████████████████

A description of this poem is not available because of the poem's robots.txt

If I lower my chin, prop my arm, turn my head, shut my mouth, and
angle the camera from above, I might look okay in a headshot. If this is a
book you should check the back cover.

They did not tell us the Declaration of Independence was a manifesto.
Fear of communist contamination. Manifestos as bedtime stories
encourage bedtime boycotts. The Fathers weren't sure if the act of
declaring made America independent or if it required additional
paperwork.

*As conditions are at present constituted—you have the choice between Parasitism,*
*& Prostitution—or Negation,* says a manifesto

One way to engender world peace is to have everyone wear a nose
cozy that mimics the snout of an extinct animal. Ivory-billed here, dodo
and saber tooth there. These would produce a performative memorial
and encourage people to sniff freely in public. To reduce the formation
of animal castes, cozies would be swapped at random every month.
Also, prior to this, there would be a revolution in which the means of
production were wrenched from hands of the capitalists.

Tornado, Hurricane, Tilt-O-Whirl, Dizzy Dragon, Swizzler, Fun Slide,
Ladies' Underhanded Skillet Toss

"This t-shirt is brighter than your future" it said

We ask the time, knowing it has stopped

We rush to grow our skins thick then shed them. I track my progress line
by line. Each day a new me in the mirror asking what I've been.

Sharks eat sharks. Their bodies undulating with pleasure.

I take the pulse of a limb / ask the leaves to breathe me in

21

Unknot dream from thought. Bedsheets tangled at my feet.

The dermatologist said I was okay wrinkle-wise but not pigment-wise

For two weeks I've carried around a plastic six-pack top, unable to cut it, unable to throw it away

I try to dissolve my edges but cannot find the perimeter. A bruised thigh becomes synecdoche for *my*.

I try to reclaim my time

There is a Texas made of trash in the ocean

*Here the manuscript breaks off,* said someone

Sharing the labor of meaning making, we make nothing again and again

How old must I be / how many degrees do I need to inoculate myself against the condescension of men?

Women often shame each other for taking too long on the toilet. This is where organic repression meets patriarchy.

Invasive species as botanical xenophobia

The caterpillar letting the wind sway its silk as a politics

I would like to talk about family but our story is silence

A man's eyes on me / slick rock / river between my thighs

I turn it over: / yes, there was another / yes, you were the wronged one // I build the scene anew each day / I say I say I stay

Your hands on my page, my words in your mouth

Smoke blurs our animal scent // we make ash out of everything / we make world out of ending

22

Predawn undone

I have seen a man gutted / I have been the one to gut him

I blacked out for an entire year

It is not uncommon to want your life to splinter, to have it worry someone's hand

Turning away from my shadow to know the angle of the sun

*I am an archeologist of morning,* said someone

My mother calls and asks for advice

I learn you through a gap in the trees. Your life a cloud on the horizon.

Water pools then falls then falls then pools

Symptom of longing

You must make a monument to everything that comes your way: to lover, to tide, to cup full of wine. To the aching, the breaking, the making over again.

Grit in my teeth / I wait for pearl

They caught it early / it's growing slowly / experimental trial / optimistic outlook / she's a fighter

Some say every line should be a surprise, but sometimes the making is
enough

He thought it was only back pain. He lay down. He wasn't even 30.

I write into sleep / my mind a pool / of making

I AM STRANGERS ONCE MORE

23

Inside the fold, nerves bundled & taut

I've forgotten the shape of his back but not his mouth. This is not a sign
of longing but a side-effect of him always telling me what to want to be.

I thought if I made you work for it, you wouldn't

Other people don't seem to mind being photographed in their bathing
suits

My grandmother wanted to when I was a teenager. I said no. She said
drop dead.

Memorial bench covered in bird shit

I told her I didn't eat meat so she handed me chicken

I think I want child(ren) but they're bad for the climate

She grew up during the Depression with a stepfather who drank and
touched. I didn't know that then.

My mother made her apologize

The therapist is frustrated we can't trace it to a single childhood trauma.
It's atmospheric, I say.

I wait for news of yous

I am a person, which is to say, someone has defined my borders

I too have measured the gap between my thighs

I really want you to like my poems

After all these years imagining pain, I finally made it real

For instance, the rabbit only speaks at death in order to warn its kin

Bodies in conversation / the heat between

24

Song in my mouth

I won't apologize for writing sad poems, which have gone viral on tumblr, she said

The you I'm talking to is ionized

I almost loved someone because I loved the sound of my words in his mouth. I realized before it was too too late that I was just learning to love myself.

It began, as all things do, in a garden

Draw a circle around anything and you will find the inside means

Love me in the mean time

Most cat videos are erotic. As in, if you filmed two humans licking each other's faces and wearing collars it would be blocked from Instagram.

Several entrepreneurs have started following me on Twitter. Poems a sound investment.

Application for NASA's Planetary Protection Office position aka alien ambassador

They already live among us

I've noticed the days start and end poetically. Prose in the meantime.

The small touches under tables, the gentle glances. Heart in my throat, heat in my gut.

Sun through my eyelids. Red as my mouth on yours.

I perform the ritual cleansing. I erase each letter of his too-short name. I unsay unsay unstay.

Like me a little lonely please

Contain me. I fear my effects.

I WAIT FOR A POEM TO WAKE ME / I ACHE FOR A POEM TO MAKE ME

25

Eyes of wood, mouth of water. Steam me open.

The meaning of it all, after all

When earth becomes fuel for the sun in 5 billion years. Solar powered.

Just because I'm PMSing doesn't mean it isn't real

This requires more effort than you'd think. A constant waking.

I don't know how to stop. I did not design an exit plan.

Every mechanism has a failsafe: failure a part of its routine function

Fraudulent clicks being a main concern

For example, the failsafe on the Deepwater Horizon failed

Every day I consent to the death of others so I can live. How I live with it.

*The practice of the poem is the practice of radical materiality*, said someone

I count the seconds between light and breaking

Heat rises from wet gravel

It is a matter of time and a time of matter

210 millions Gallons gushed into the Gulf of Mexico. That's over 4 million bathtubs.

It is hard to archive. A dreg in the ocean. Drag of bodies along the shore. Business returns, contrary to local reports of the dark taste in the water. Gills filled with it.

Mistakes were made after midnight

My procedure protected me

26

Sandpaper eyes & half-mumbled goodbyes

The people form a united front against delays but turn against each other come cancellation

My body is read

One flight cancelled, another delayed

A FL man next to shows me unsolicited photos. Sublime landscapes with lots of filter. "Disney World brought the scum to Orlando," he says. "Had to pull a gun on someone and I didn't even want to." He spreads his legs and falls asleep.

The birds and me in the airport

Chris Nelson wrote a book of poems about being in an airport. It begins with shout-outs to all his friends, which accentuates the loneliness of airportness.

Scully Levi Diana Elise Arianna Linnea Curtis Rachael Steph Gothmog James Geoff Jeff Leah Trevors

"I understood that everyone around me was waiting / for flights that never departed," he says

My flight is always 3 hours away

Platinum / Magnum / Opus / Emerald / Gold / Silver / Bronze / Business / The People

I grew up near Disney Land. The fantasy did not last long. Hot lines and my thighs sticking to everything. The voices I kept turning toward that weren't addressing me.

*The stone, not the mind, draws / circles in the pond*, said someone. A mantra for airport tranquility.

The iPad installed at the charging station flashes an image of the chip bag I am holding. I watch the machine watch me.

We swarm the tunnel, faces warm with annunciation

I remove my shoes and fold my body

/

/

I was asleep

I don't have much patience for the plot of *Dazed & Confused*. The boy becoming a man is a trope that needs no more telling.

We applaud & sleep-shuffle

Against the apparition of the crowd / a face I love without knowing how

I DIG A HOLE IN THE SAND / OF OUR SORROW // I CRAWL INSIDE /
WANTING / A WAVE TO BURY ME

**APPENDIX A**: Surplus Lines Written Between Time

A burial creates the illusion of resolve

A man I've met four times just pointed at me and said: "I DON'T KNOW WHO YOU ARE!"

Averages cast a shadow over things which are already dark

Before the flood, we made silt with our tears

But what can I possibly say, knowing my mother might someday read it?

Day thief, you hide behind the trees. Wait for sun to cede.

Do you worry how age hangs on your hips? Passenger of time who watches through the rearview.

Every morning I see a man who looks like Santa. I smile; he nods.

Fact: You can't actually "dispose" of nuclear waste

Fish with no eyes / Spiders without legs / children with no hands

Fog thick as dog breath in my ear

"Freedom of Information Act"

Geopolitics or gender?

Get what you need by not asking for it

Holistically hostile host

Hungry hungry Kristin

I call this the JFK residency

I remove the atmosphere and evacuate its residue. I excavate the future.

I cannot get outside my ruin

I cut my throat on this morning's melancholy and wish my heart would too

I don't think I'm being dramatic when I say it's only a matter of time until I have cancer

I don't think this poem can learn from its mistakes

I eat a hunk of cheese and wait for small plane to take me to a larger one

I am my own stenographer

I might need to start censoring myself

"I'm not trying to be rude" is not a good way to start a conversation

I never called my mother back. Will try today (update: failed).

I put a chip in my cat but it did not help me find her when she ran away

I will never add you to my LinkedIn network

I'm all surface, but I'm a dodecahedron

It did allow them to call me when they found her body later, though

Language is not arbitrary. There are material conditions and family systems.

Lightning in the cloud next to mine

Looking for your mother in someone else's face

Many still set the aesthetic against the political

Method to hypnotize a shark: tickle its snout

Mine is the last to emerge

My urine tells me to drink more water

No bottom to the explanation, no discoverable limit

Open air binds a wound. Winds tight the skin that breaks and breaks.

Punishing the symptom, we sleep a little better.

*Remember you are nothing without credit,* said C.D. Wright

Shape of a mouth saying / grip of a hand on my wrist

Silhouettes on the screen merge then break apart, return to the start

Swallow the barium and see the passages your body hoards. All the paths you could have taken. All the ways to be made.

Take my picture

The apple is obsolete / it schedules its own obsolescence

They bequeathed their 666,000 gallons of high-level nuclear waste to the state by burying it inside its belly

This poem is not about method

This poem is not an object

This whole town smells of skunk

Treble of your tongue through the wire. Tentacular love makes living fragile.

Unproductive analogies make language an obtuse object

What I lack in beauty I try to make up for in brains, I always say to no one

I am thinking of a trace. The erotic atomic face.

What is the meaning of being humorless?

You should know I'm not taking any shortcuts. I write each segment in pencil and then transcribe it on a computer.

You look at your phone. I look at you.

Your love is clearer than a shadow at noon

**APPENDIX B**: Index of Said Someones

4
*Certain stones which have the figures of animals inside and outside*
—Albertus Magnus

*Identity is a wound*
—Eirini Avramopoulou

5
*The soul is the form of a natural body which potentially has life*
—Albertus Magnus

6
*What happens to water and earth also happens to animals and plants, since by a hidden power of material, the time, or the place, they are completely disintegrated or converted into stone*
—Albertus Magnus

*A self-organizing system feeds upon noise*
—Jasper Bernes

*Who gets to live a livable life?*
—Eirini Avramopoulou

9
I first heard the phrase "living a making" in an artist talk by Nayland Blake.

11
*A mutation occurs when the ionization of an atom changes the genetic coding of a cell, producing a new reproductive outcome.*
—Joseph Masco

12
*Omne vivum ex vivo:* "all life is from life"
—Louis Pasteur

13
*My mother is a fish.*
—Vardaman Bundren in *As I Lay Dying* by William Faulkner

14
*Matter without place*
*—Peter Van Wyck*

See information on Hanford radionuclides from Washington State Dept. of Health report, archived here:https://web.archive.org/web/20100812054326/ http://www.doh.wa.gov/hanford/publications/history/release.html#Green

*While smaller releases have continued since 1972, the Congressional mandate for the Hanford Health Information Network (HHIN) limits the Network to providing information about the releases of radioactive materials from 1944 to 1972*
—Washington State Dept. of Health

*To date, there has been no practical need for a final HLW repository*
—The World Nuclear Association

15
*We want to return it to a safe state…We promised the local people that we would recover the site and make it a safe ground again*
—Yuichi Okamura, general manager of the Tokyo electric's nuclear power and plant siting division

*A permanent ration of collective standardized poisoning*
—Ulrich Beck

18
*Hell no, we won't glow*
—Antinuclear chant used in the 70s.

"Once or twice in her life / a woman is gutted / like a fish" is after Ilya Kaminsky's poem "Musica Humana" in *Dancing in Odessa:* "Once or twice in his life, a man / is peeled like apples."

17
"Who sang the sorrows of whose changing face" is after William Butler Yeats's "When You Are Old":"But one man loved the pilgrim soul in you, / And loved the sorrows of your changing face."

20
*As conditions are at present constituted—you have the choice between Parasitism, &*
*Prostitution—or Negation*
—Mina Loy

21
*Here the manuscript breaks off*
—Frederic Engels

22
*I am an archeologist of morning*
—Charles Olson

25
*The practice of the poem is the practice of radical materiality,* said someone
—Miyung Mi Kim

26
*The stone, not the mind, draws / circles in the pond*
—Tomaž Šalamun